This Handwriting Notebook
Belongs To:

A

A is For

B is For

C is For

D is For

E is For

F is For

G

G is For

H is For

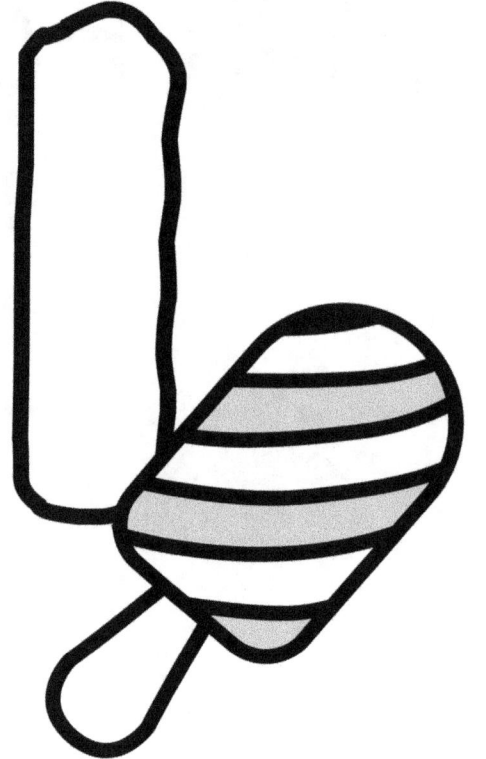

I is For

J

J is For

K is For

L is For

M is For

N is For

O is For

P

P is For

Q is For

Q is For

R

R is For

S is For

T is For

U is For

V is For

W is For

X is For

Y

Y is For

Y is For

Z is For

www.ingramcontent.com/pod-product-compliance
Lightning Source LLC
Chambersburg PA
CBHW060103070526
44654CB00051B/1612